Basic Chord Const

Major Triad - *Consists of three intervals, the root, 3rd, and 5th.*

Minor Triad - *The 3rd interval is lowered 1/2 step (1 key).*

Diminished - *Chords with all intervals a minor 3rd apart. (2 keys between each note)*

Augmented - *5th interval is raised 1/2 step. (1 key)*

Sixth - *6th interval is added to the major triad.*

Minor Sixth - *3rd interval of the 6th chord is lowered 1/2 step. (1 key)*

Seventh - *Consists of 4 intervals, the root, 3rd, 5th and flatted 7th.*

Minor Seventh - *3rd interval of the 7th chord is lowered 1/2 step. (1 key)*

Ninth - *Consists of the 5 intervals, the root, 3rd, 5th, flatted 7th, and 9th.*

Intervals

An interval is the distance between two notes, as the diagram illustrates.

Inversions

The various positions of each chord are called inversions. A chord is inverted to place it in a position that can be played more comfortably. When inverting a chord, the bottom note is moved up an octave, becoming the top note and creating a new inversion of the chord. The following illustrates the process of the C Major Triad.

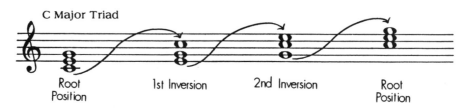

The number of inversions possible is limited only by the number of notes in the chord.

For ease of playing with the left hand, this book pictures some inversions. These chords are noted with an asterisk, and the root position is shown in the treble clef notation.

To play the chords for both hands (pictured on pages 28 - 33) with one hand, simply eliminate the root. Inversion may be necessary to play comfortably.

How To Use This Book

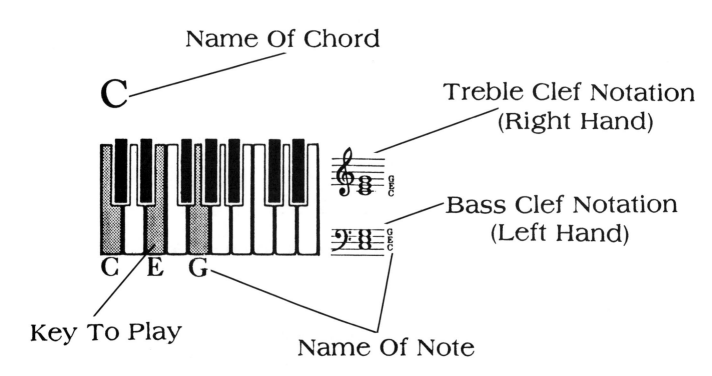

Left Hand Accompaniment Patterns

The following examples are basic left-handed accompaniment patterns illustrated below in a popular chord progression.

Block chord

Drone, or open fifths

Broken chord in 2

Broken chord in 3

Broken chord in 4

Broken chord, Alberti bass

Arpeggio in 2

Arpeggio in 3

Arpeggio in 4

Arpeggio in 6

Arpeggiated, or rolled chords

C Chords

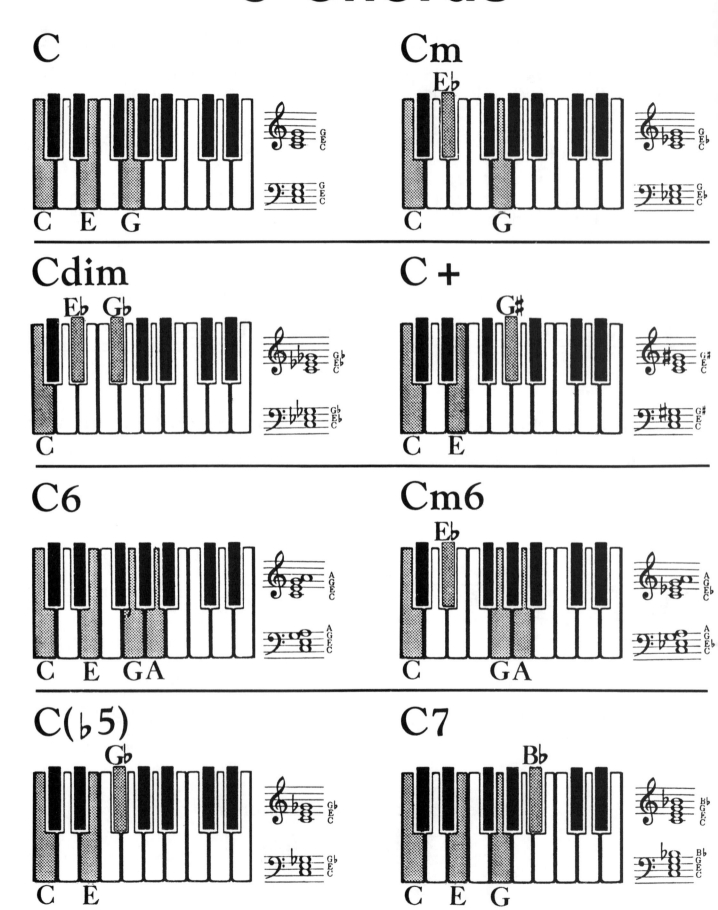

C Chords

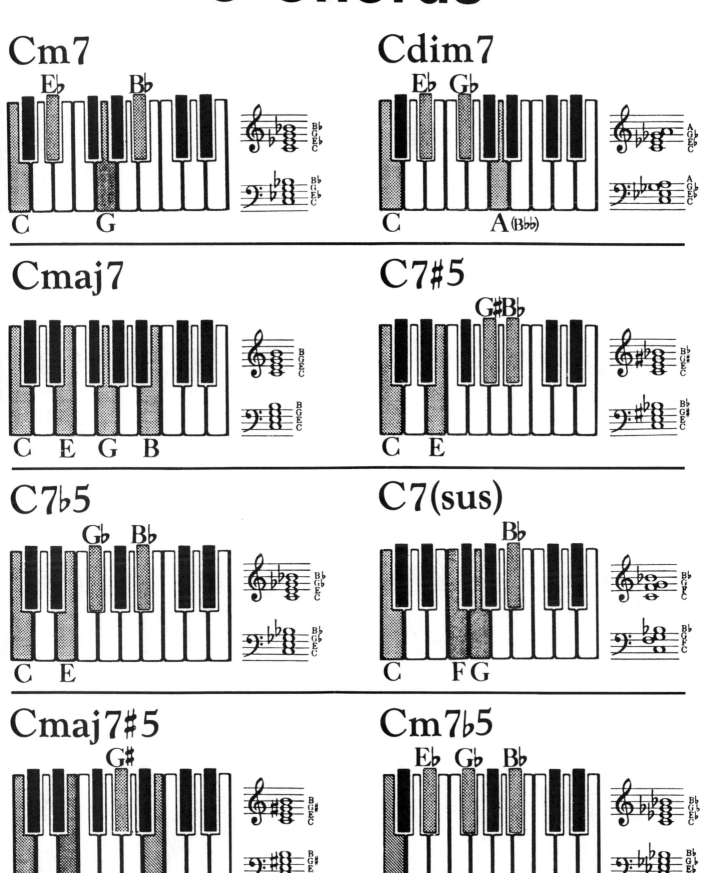

D♭ (C♯) Chords

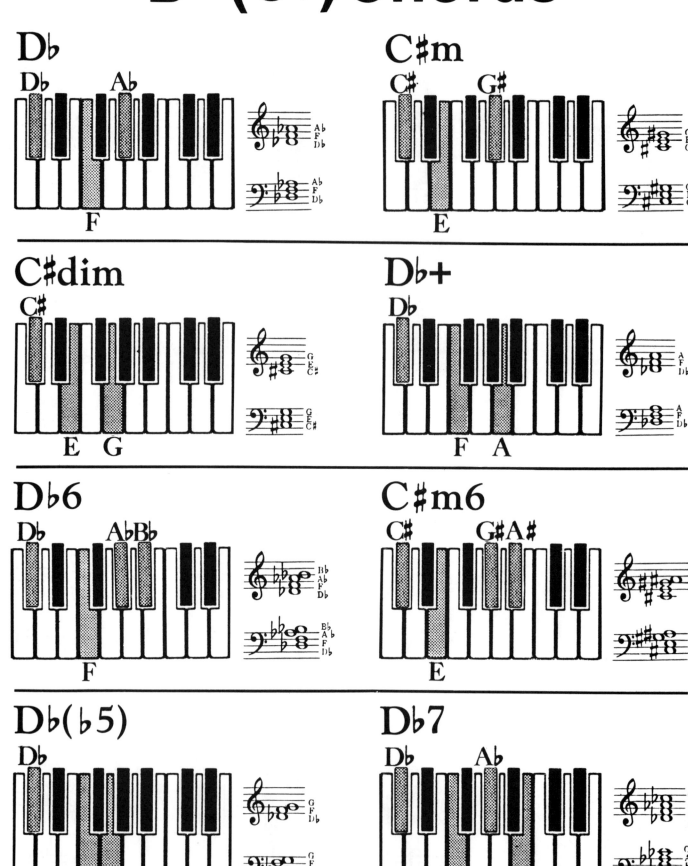

Db (C#) Chords

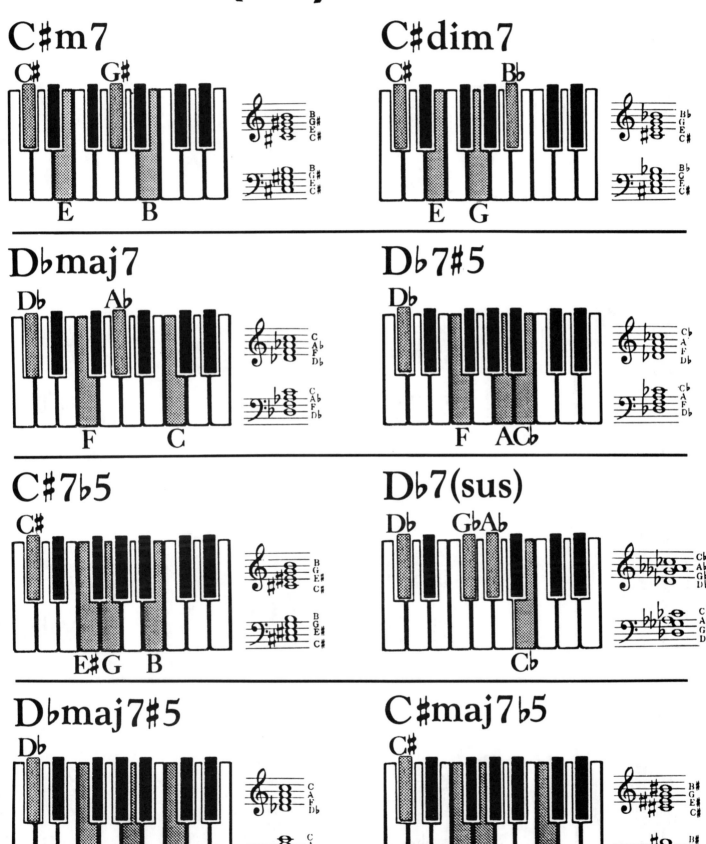

D Chords

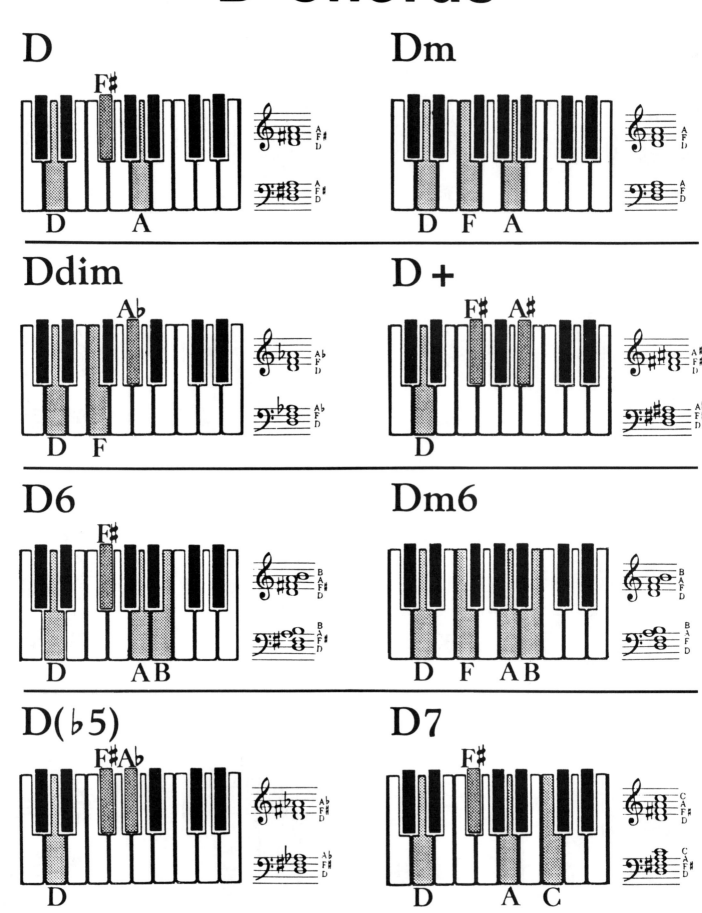

D Chords

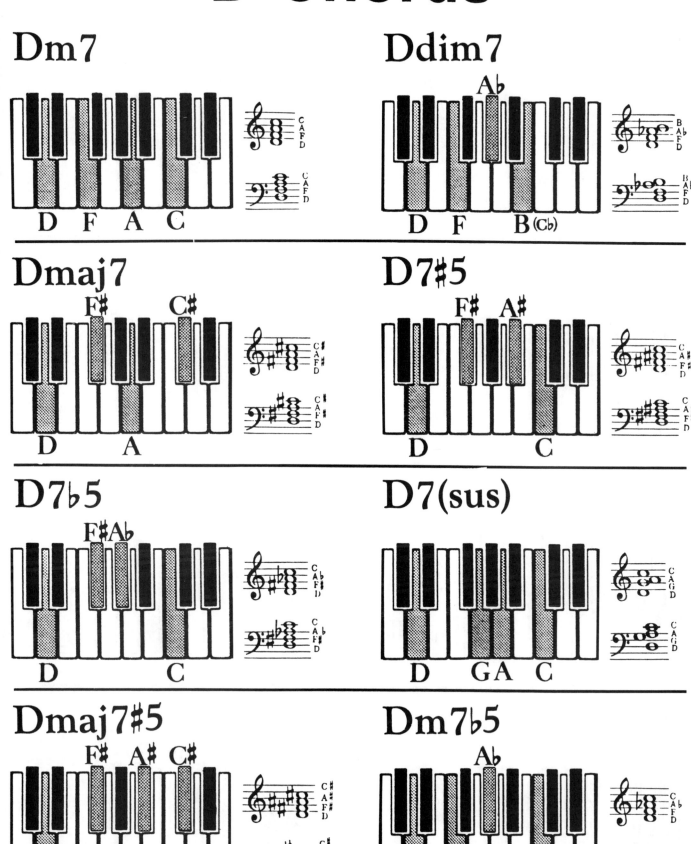

E♭ Chords

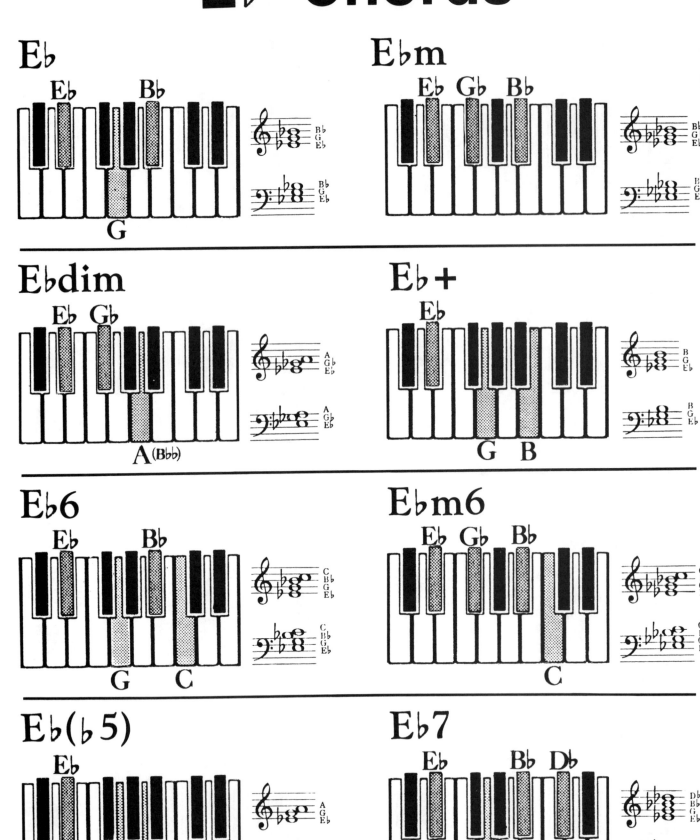

E♭ Chords

E♭m7

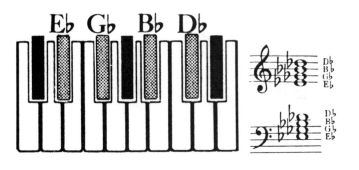

E♭dim7

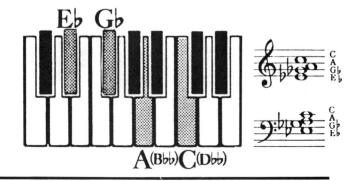

E♭maj7

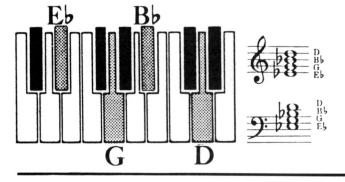

E♭7♯5

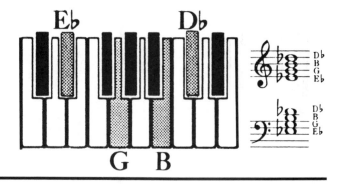

E♭7♭5

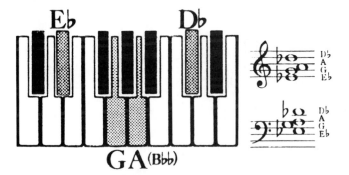

E♭7(sus)

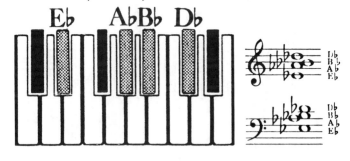

E♭maj7♯5

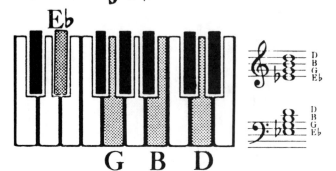

E♭m7♭5

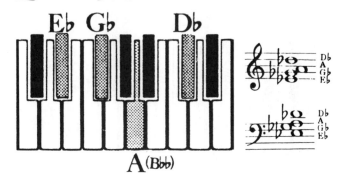

E Chords

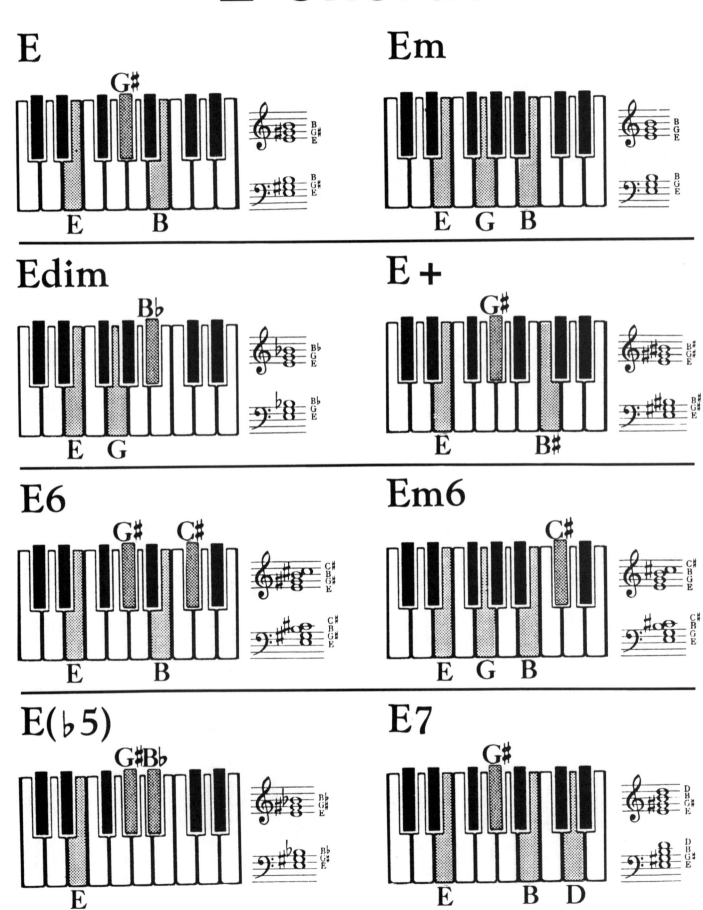

E Chords

Em7
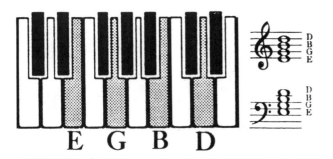

Edim7
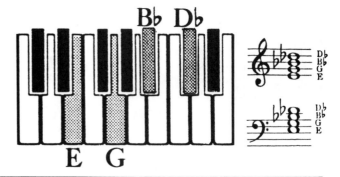

Emaj7
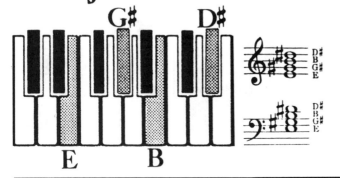

E7#5
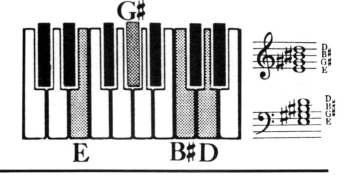

E7♭5
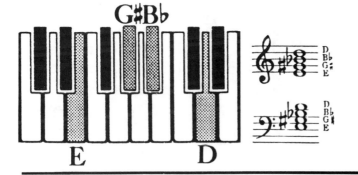

E7(sus)
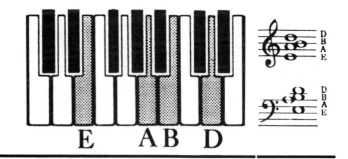

Emaj7#5
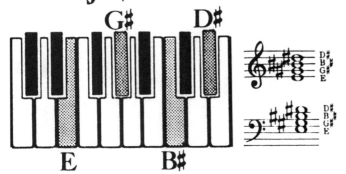

Em7♭5
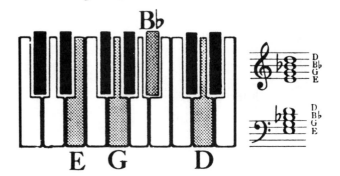

F Chords

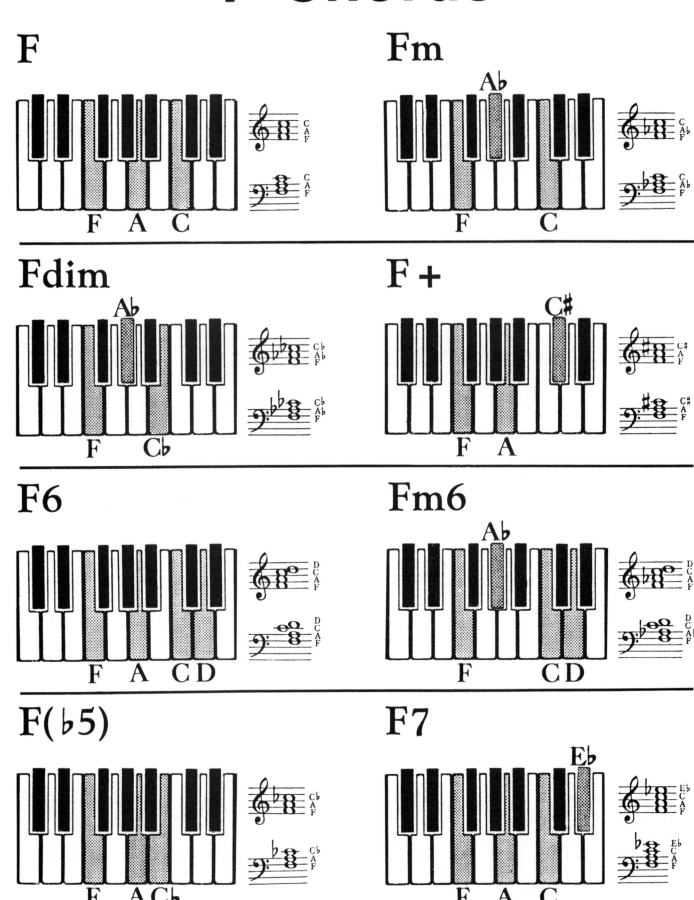

F Chords

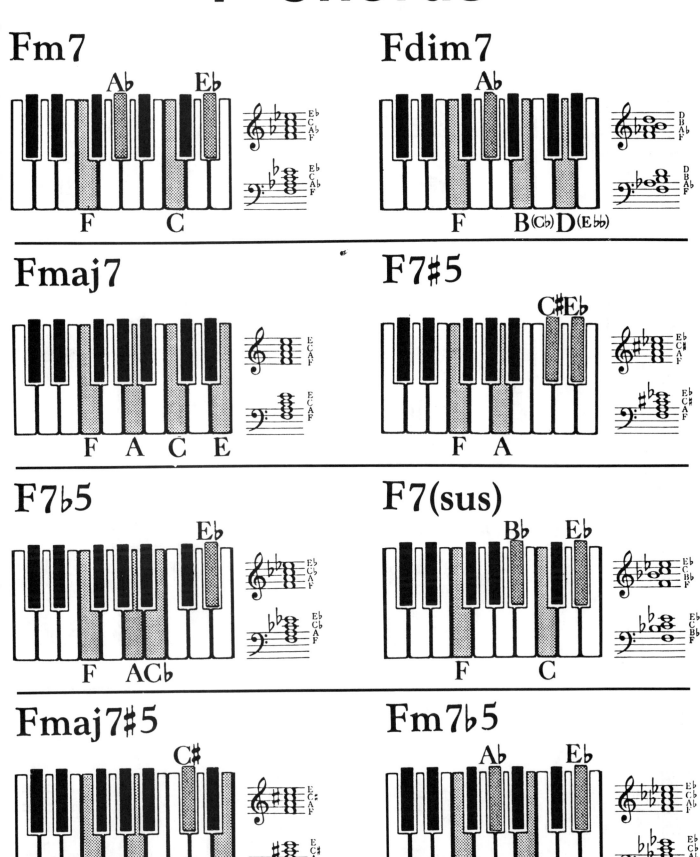

F# (G♭) Chords

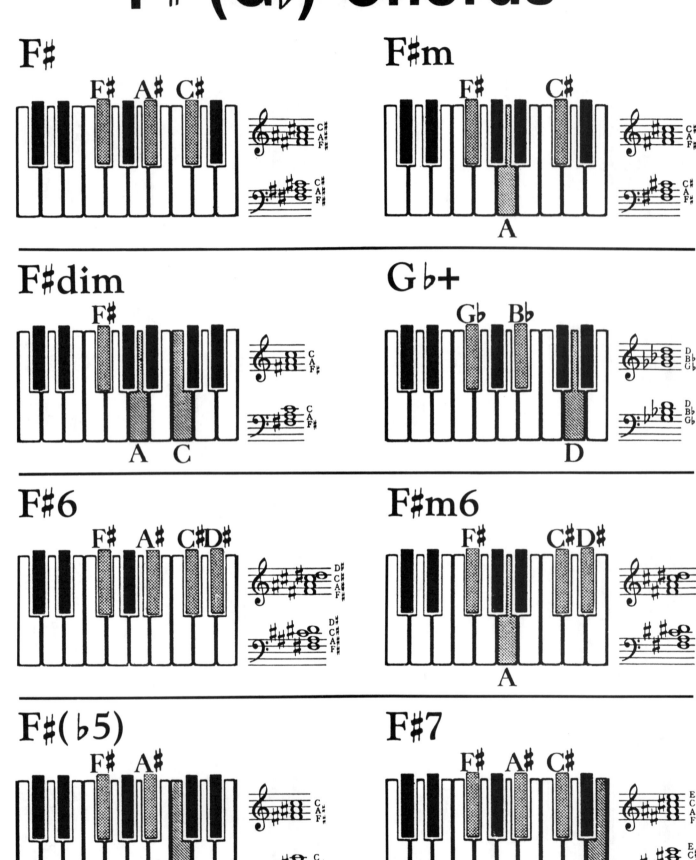

♯ (G♭) Chords

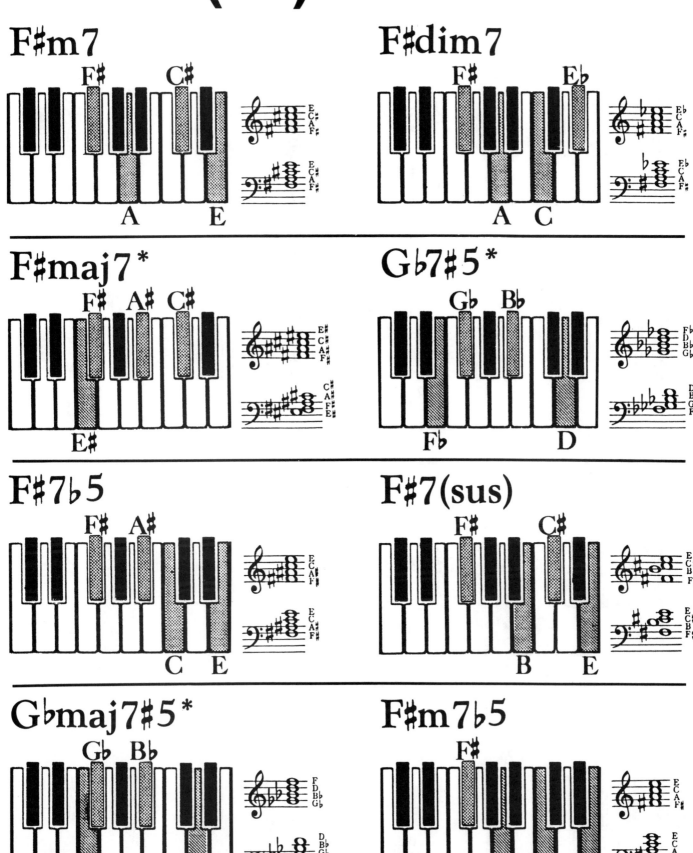

F♯m7

F♯dim7

F♯maj7 *

G♭7♯5 *

F♯7♭5

F♯7(sus)

G♭maj7♯5 *

F♯m7♭5

*Inversion see page 2

17

G Chords

G
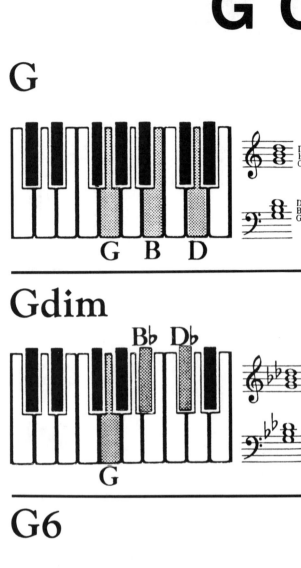
G B D

Gm
Bb
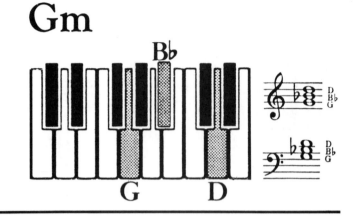
G D

Gdim
Bb Db
G

G +
D#
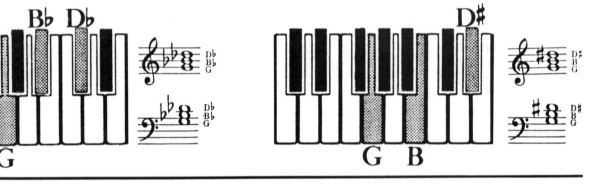
G B

G6
G B D E

Gm6
Bb
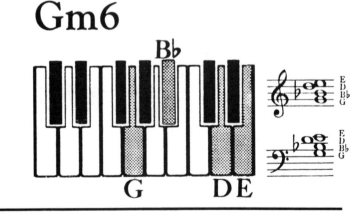
G D E

G(b5)
Db
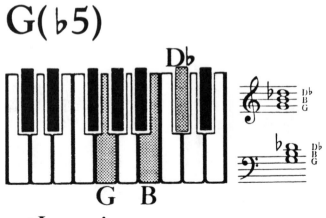
G B

G7 *
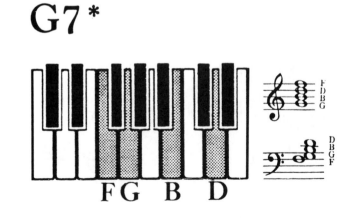
F G B D

*Inversion see page 2

18

G Chords

Gm7*
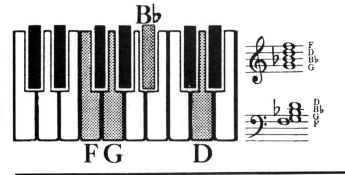

Gdim7
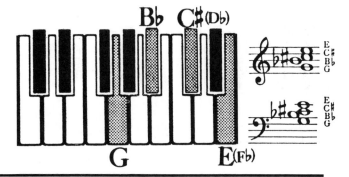

Gmaj7*
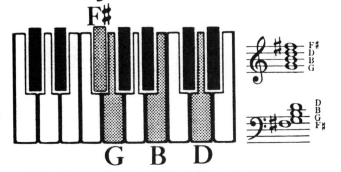

G7#5*
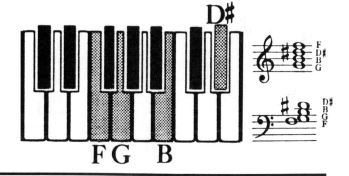

G7b5 *
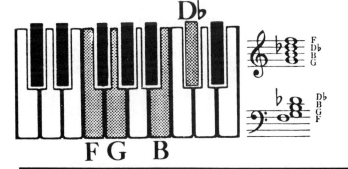

G7(sus)*
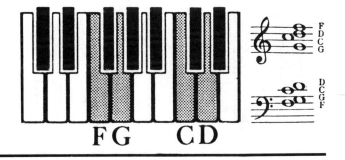

Gmaj7#5 *
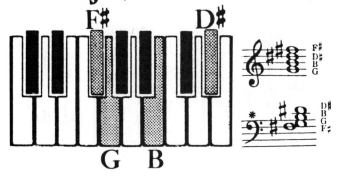

Gm7b5 *
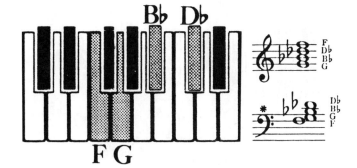

*Inversion see page 2

19

A♭ Chords

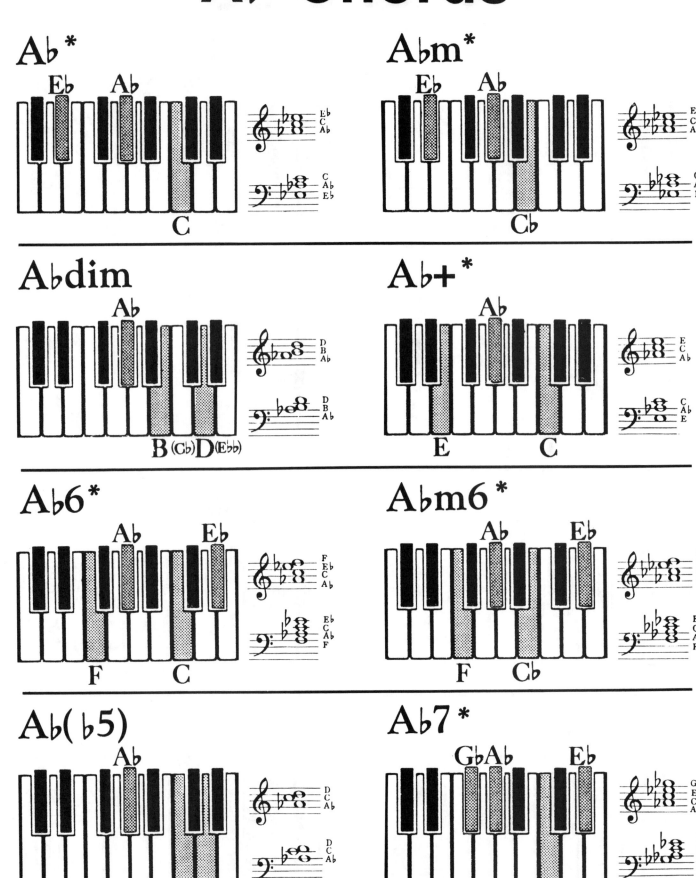

A♭ Chords

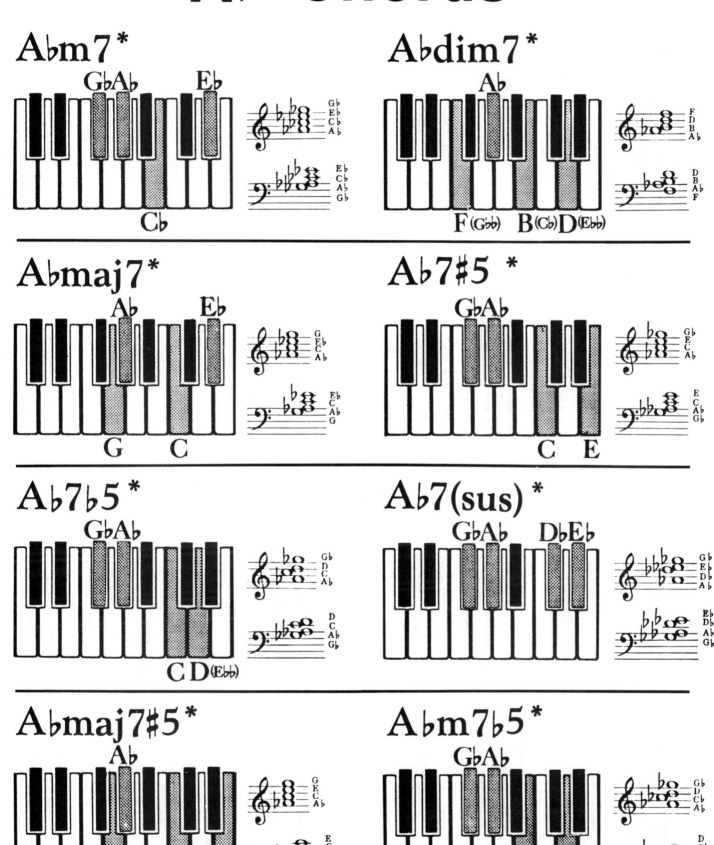

Abm7*

Abdim7*

Abmaj7*

Ab7#5 *

Ab7b5 *

Ab7(sus) *

Abmaj7#5*

Abm7b5 *

*Inversion see page 2

21

A Chords

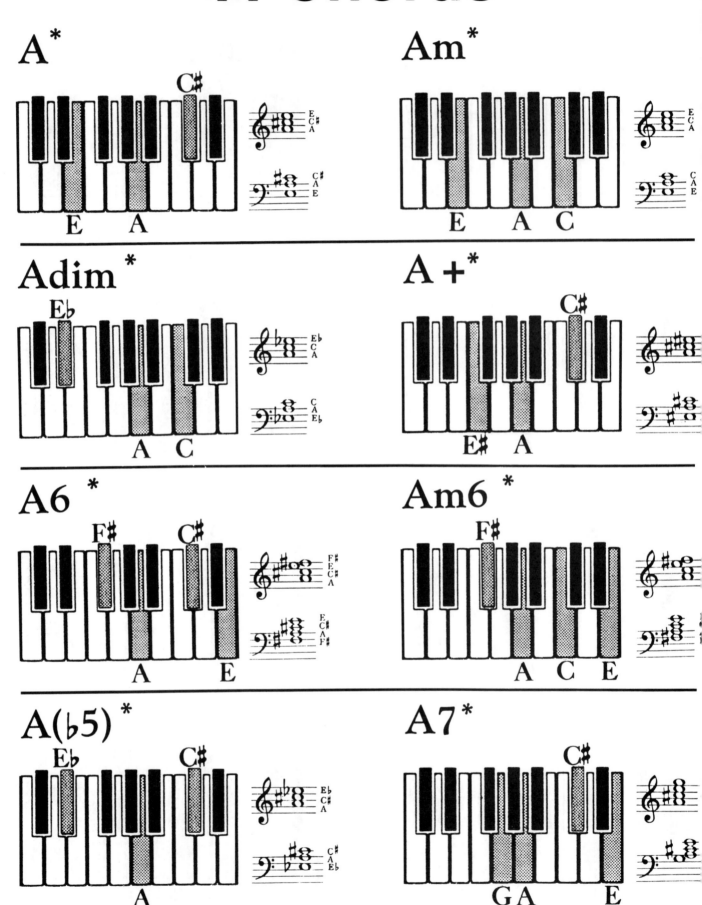

A*

Am*

Adim*

A+*

A6*

Am6*

A(♭5)*

A7*

*Inversion see page 2

22

A Chords

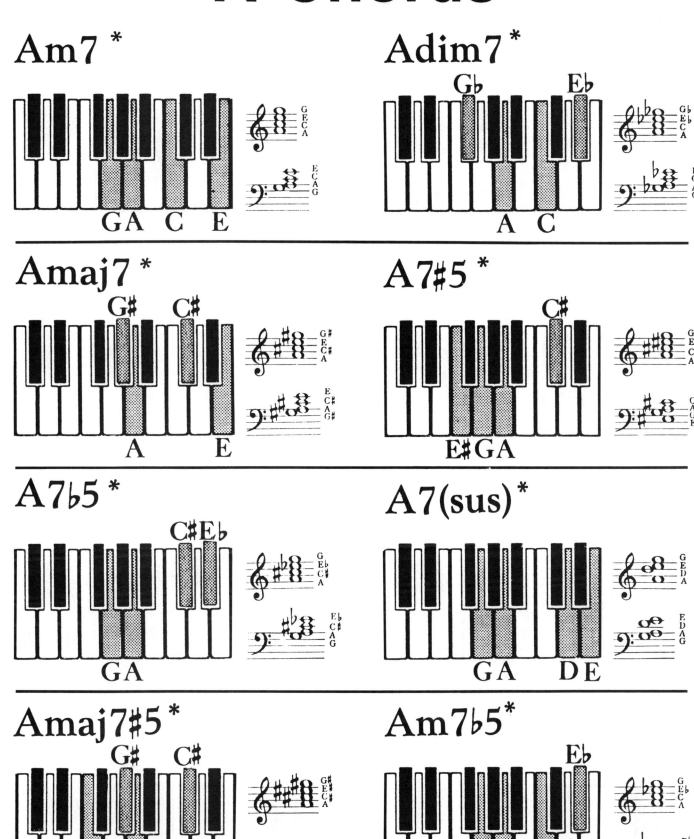

Am7 *

Adim7 *

Amaj7 *

A7#5 *

A7♭5 *

A7(sus) *

Amaj7#5 *

Am7♭5 *

*Inversion see page 2

23

B♭ Chords

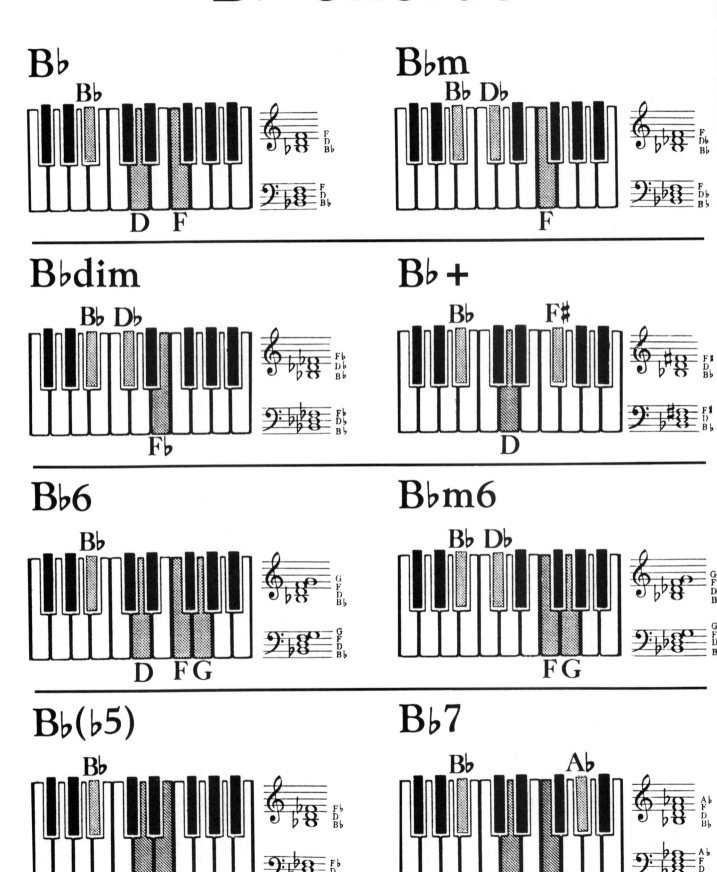

B♭ Chords

B♭m7

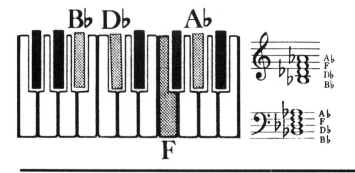

B♭dim7

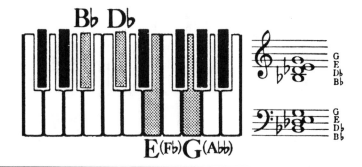

B♭maj7

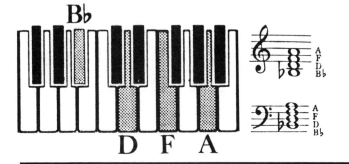

B♭7♯5

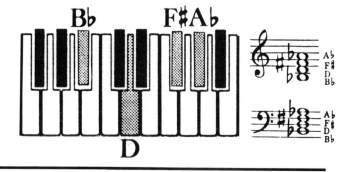

B♭7♭5

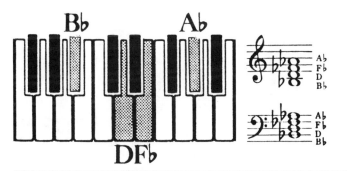

B♭7(sus)

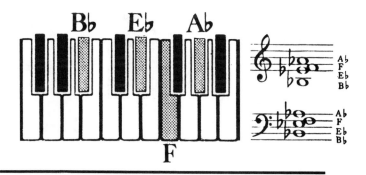

B♭maj7♯5

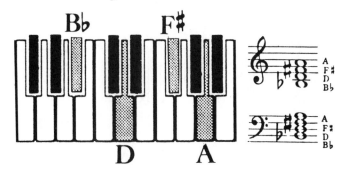

B♭m7♭5

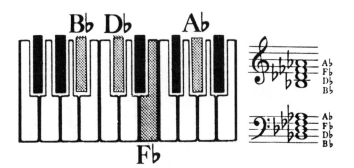

B Chords

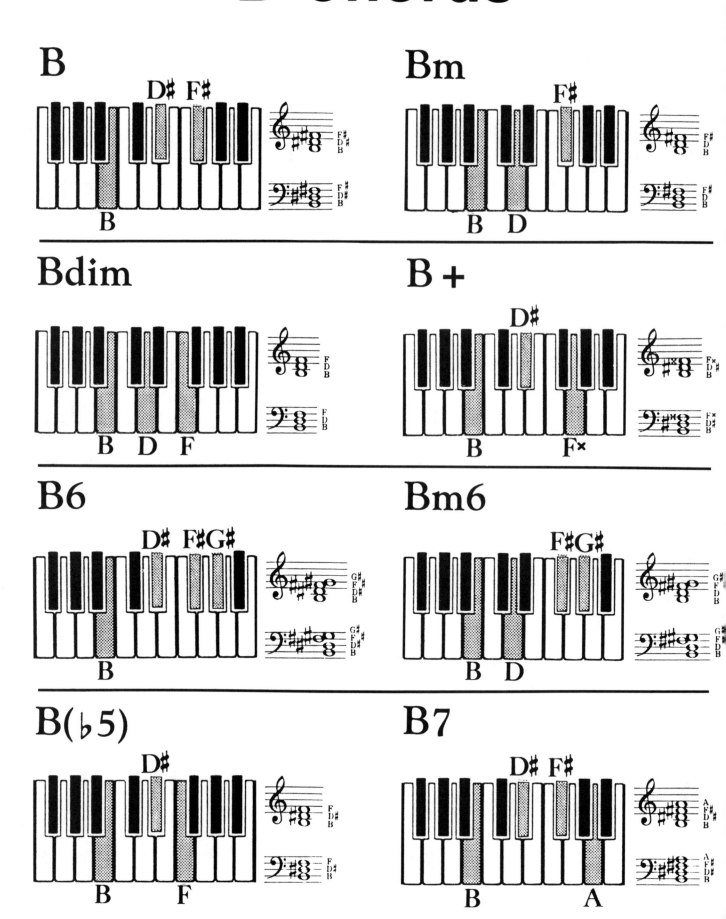

B Chords

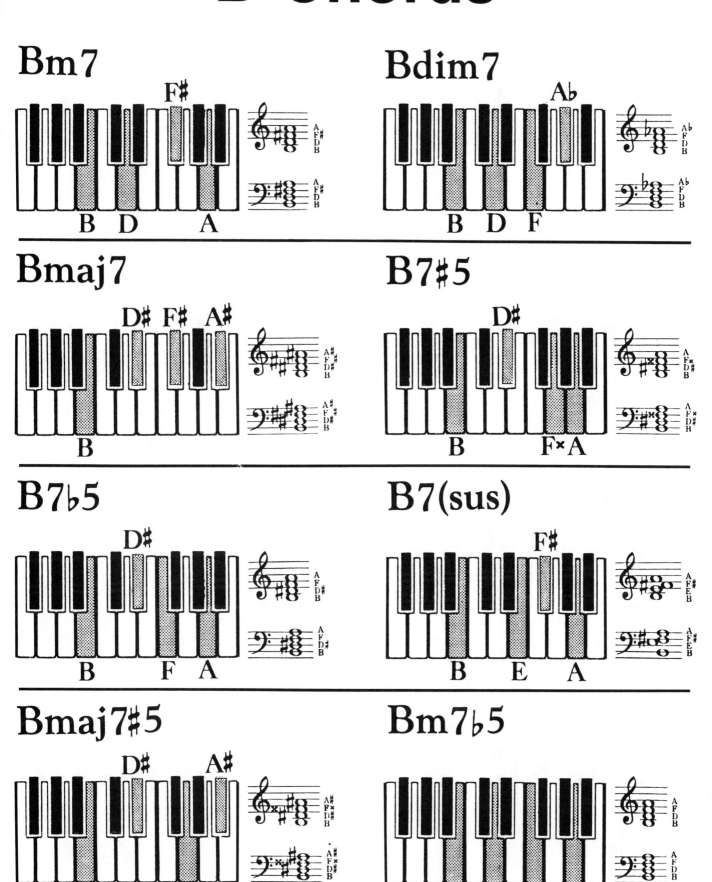

C/D♭ Chords For Both Hands

see page 2 (inversions)

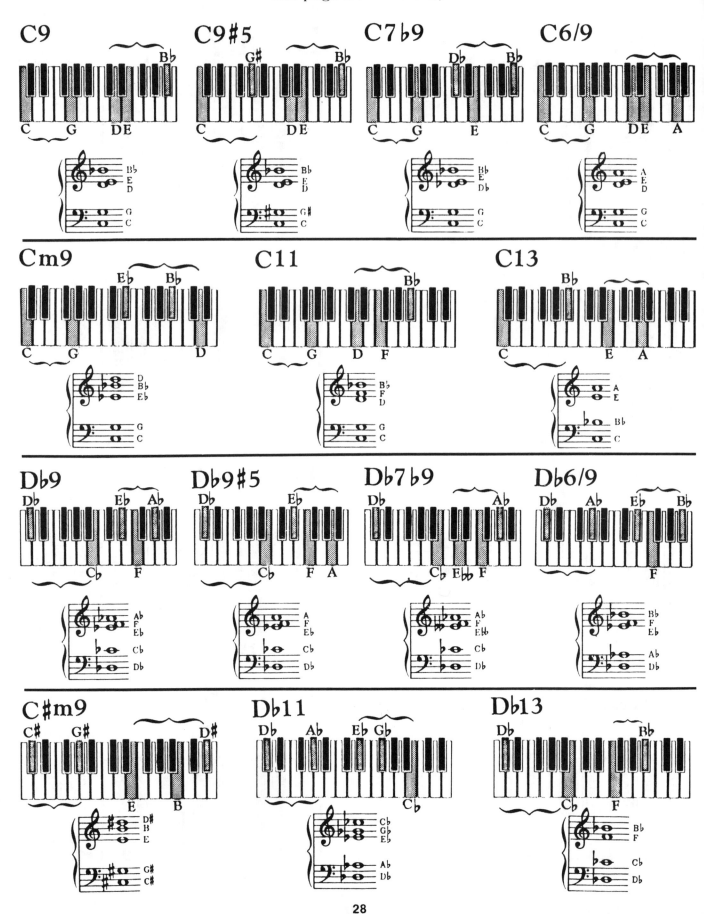

D/E♭ Chords For Both Hands

see page 2 (inversions)

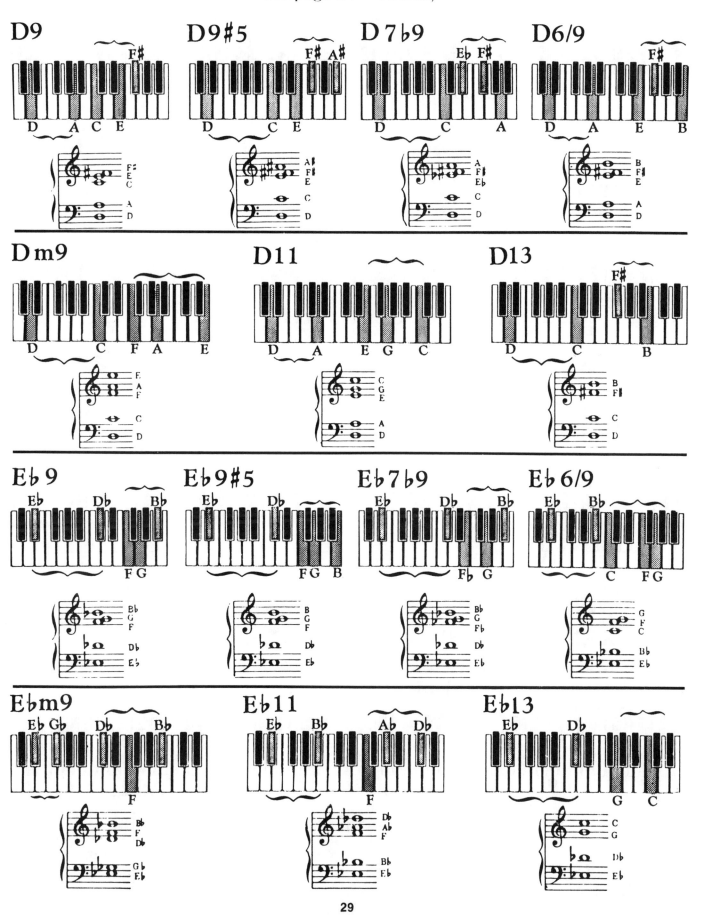

29

E/F Chords For Both Hands

see page 2 (inversions)

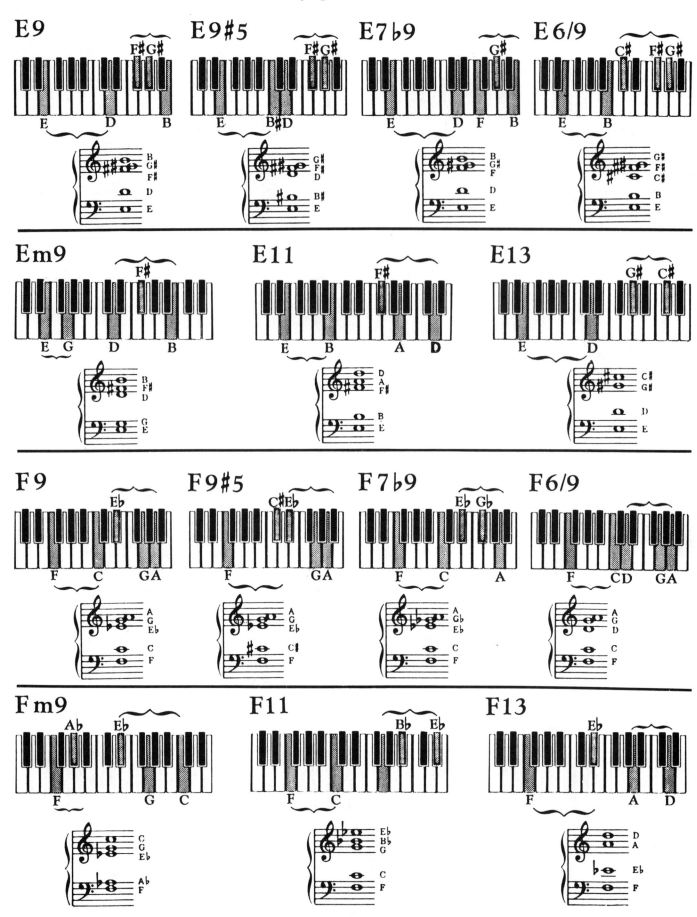

F♯/G Chords For Both Hands

see page 2 (inversions)

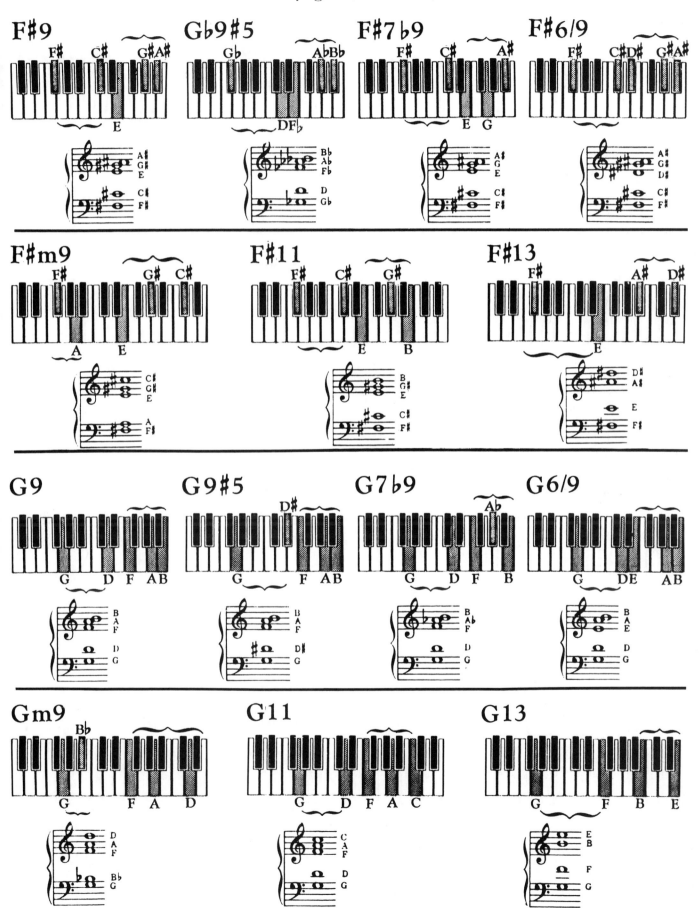

31

A♭/A Chords For Both Hands

see page 2 (inversions)

A♭9
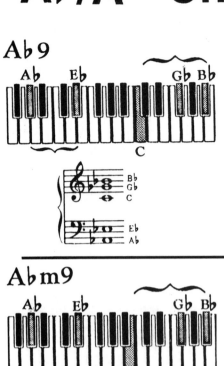

A♭9#5
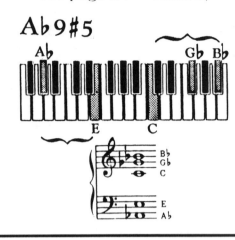

A♭7♭9
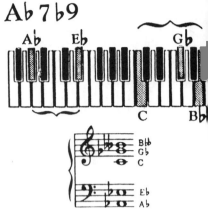

A♭m9
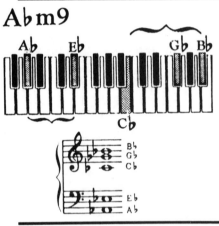

A♭11
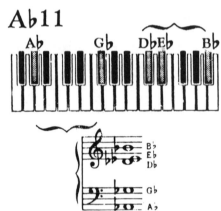

A♭13
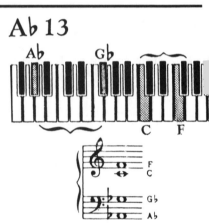

A9
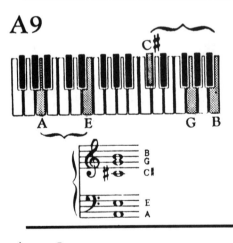

A9#5
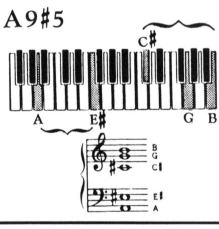

A7♭9
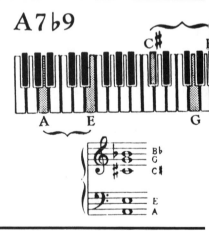

Am9
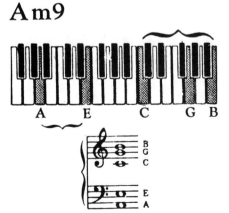

A11
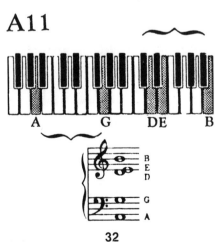

A13
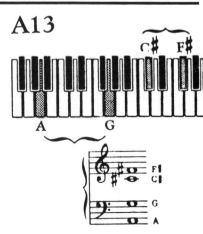